From Living a Nightmare to Walking With Angels

By Bill Givler

TEACH Services, Inc.
PUBLISHING
www.TEACHServices.com • (800) 367-1844

ISBN-13: 978-1-4796-0355-8 (Paperback)
ISBN-13: 978-1-4796-0356-5 (ePub)
ISBN-13: 978-1-4796-0357-2 (Mobi)
Library of Congress Control Number: 2014944870

Published by

TEACH Services, Inc.
PUBLISHING
www.TEACHServices.com • (800) 367-1844

A true story
about a young boy's journey
from spiritual harassment
to finding the Lord,
to walking with angels.

Contents

Introduction

It is my sincere desire that this book will guide you to God's Word and to our Lord and Savior, Jesus Christ. Christ is our only hope for deliverance from this dark world of the supernatural.

Some may question the events that happened in my life, but I know I'm not the only one who has had supernatural experiences. I could share many more experiences with you, but I want to focus on God's Word. For many years I blocked these events out of my mind, for I didn't want to think of them. I only wanted to keep God's Word before me after leaving the dark side behind. However, I believe God has impressed me to help others that they too may be delivered from this world of spiritual darkness and brought to the light of the Word and Jesus Christ.

As you read this book, invite God's presence through the Holy Spirit to be with you, for if you do, He will guide you and protect you:

Submit yourselves therefore to God. Resist the devil, and he will flee from you. Draw nigh to God, and he will draw nigh to you. Cleanse your hands, ye sinners; and purify your hearts, ye double minded. Be afflicted, and mourn, and weep: let your laughter be turned to mourning, and your joy to heaviness. Humble yourselves in the sight of the Lord, and he shall lift you up. (James 4:7–10)

Let your conversation be without covetousness; and be content with such things as ye have: for he hath said, I will never leave thee, nor forsake thee. So that we may boldly say, The Lord is my helper, and I will not fear what man shall do unto me. (Heb. 13:5, 6)

And I will pray the Father, and he shall give you another Comforter, that he may abide with you forever; ... But the Comforter, which is the Holy Ghost, whom the Father will send in my name, he shall teach you all things, and bring all things to your remembrance, whatsoever I have said unto you. Peace I leave with you, my peace I give unto you: not as the world giveth, give I unto you. Let not your heart be troubled, neither let it be afraid. (John 14:16, 26, 27)

Chapter 1

Living the Nightmare

I remember the stories my mother used to tell me about my grandmother, how she was a good woman, how she believed in God and went to church, and how she knew things or could sense things, such as when people died or got hurt or when something was wrong. She seemed to be able to communicate with the spirit world.

One story I remember happened when our neighbor died. He had a wood shop next door that he was always working in—you could hear him sawing wood or hammering all the time. When he died, his family locked up the shop. Then one night the saws started running. It sounded as if someone was working in the shop, but there were no lights on, and it was still locked up. My grandmother went over to the shop and called out our neighbor's name. She told him to go back to where he had come from because he didn't belong here anymore.

At that moment, everything stopped and became quiet again. My grandmother was not afraid to talk with the dead. She did it many times.

Another experience that involved my grandmother's attachment with the supernatural happened when a friend of hers was in the hospital. My grandparents went to visit her and found out that the doctors said she would be fine in a few days. However, the next day my grandmother told my grandfather that her friend had died during the night. He didn't believe her, so he called the hospital only to find out that my grandmother had been right—her friend had died. How did my grandmother know her friend had died? I remember her saying that the night her friend died little demons had jumped up and down at the end of her bed.

As a little boy, I thought these things were normal. It seemed that things like this were always happening in my grandmother's house. One day my mother told me about an experience she had had as a little girl. She said she saw a black shawl floating around the room, so she chased it, trying to catch it, but it faded into the wall. She went to the other side of the wall, but it wasn't there. This scared her so much that she prayed to God and asked Him to not let her see anything like that again, and she never did. My mother taught me that if I needed help, I could pray to God and He would answer my prayer and be there for me.

In my younger years, I went to Sunday School at various churches. It didn't seem to matter which church I went to just as long as it was a church. For me, they all seemed to teach the same things, such as that when you died you went to heaven if you were good or hell if you were bad or somewhere in between for a while. I really didn't understand all that as a child. In fact, I had questions. If you were in heaven, you were supposed to be happy, but how could you be happy looking down and seeing your loved ones hurting? Also, why would you burn forever in hell for the few mistakes you made in this short life? I was taught that God was love, but it didn't make any sense to me. How could this be love?

Church was a unique place that didn't offer much security as a child. People often spoke in tongues, and one Sunday the pastor cast out a demon from someone in church, and the demon tried to enter someone else. Everyone was jumping all over the place. My brothers, sisters, and I were all scared.

Communicating with the dead, speaking in tongues, demon possession, and casting out demons was all I knew as a child. Even though I had questions and didn't understand it, I felt everything that I saw and heard had to be true since the pastor, my grandmother, and my mother believed it, practiced it, and experienced it. Then when things started happening to me, I thought it was normal.

My first personal encounter with the supernatural world happened when I was about seven years old. I was sleeping at my grandmother's house in a little room that was just big enough for a small bed and a dresser. In the middle of the night, something woke me up. It felt as if a heavy person was sitting on my legs. It didn't hurt, but I couldn't move my legs. I couldn't see anything because the room was dark. I got scared and screamed for my mother. She came in and turned on the light. We didn't see anything, and the weight was gone from my legs. After that experience, I started sleeping with a nightlight, and everything was okay for a while.

Then one night while I was sleeping, something slapped me on the side of my face. I had my nightlight on, so I sat up in bed to see if I could see someone or something, but nothing was there. This went on for a while. I would be asleep, and then all of a sudden someone or something would slap me, but I could never see anything. One night after being slapped I turned over and looked at the wall above the head of my bed, and there was an ugly face just laughing at me. I screamed and ran out of the room. When I came back with my mom, there was nothing there. I never slept in that room again, and later I was told that my grandmother saw things in that room too.

My grandmother died when I was young, but I had been around her enough to become acquainted with her supernatural experiences and abilities. Now it seemed to me that I was the one having supernatural experiences—seeing and hearing things. I learned that if I slept in the same room with my brothers I would be all right. And I started sleeping under the covers all the time, so I wouldn't see anything. I also set up all my stuffed animals around me to protect me. I didn't want to tell any of my brothers or sisters that I was scared or what I had seen because I didn't want them to be scared. Then I started sleepwalking and waking up in different rooms. Sometimes if I woke up I'd fall over things in the dark, which was dangerous. I often asked myself why this was happening to me. Was God trying to tell me something, or was the devil mad at me because God had saved my life when I was born prematurely and when I caught pneumonia before turning one?

I stopped going to church when I was about eleven. As I entered my teen years, I was not being slapped or scared anymore because the spirits were more open to me now. Sometimes one would just come into the same room with me even if someone else was there. Some I could see, others I couldn't, but I could always feel the coldness of their presence. It's hard to explain, but I knew where they were in the room. One time a friend was with me, and we prayed for God's presence to be with us, and the front door opened and shut three times. I guess three demons left the house that night.

One night something woke me up in the middle of the night. My room was dark, but I could see light coming through my window from outside. As I looked at the window, I could see an outline of a woman standing outside, even though my room was upstairs. She called me over to the window for she said she wanted to show me something. Her voice was beautiful. It was comforting and peaceful. As I looked out the window she showed me signs of three deaths and warned me, in God's name, to not live as dangerously as I had been. I'd climb on mountain cliffs about one to two hundred feet off the ground without ropes; I'd explore caves or cracks formed by earthquakes.

As I was looking out the window at this spirit being, my sister ran into the room and grabbed me. She said she thought I was going to jump out the window. I told her I wasn't going to jump, but that a spirit or maybe an angel was talking to me and showing me things. I didn't recognize the source of the messages and believed that God was trying to tell me something.

Now that I was older the supernatural fascinated me, and although the devil was behind all of this, I thought that if the message was good or something good happened to me, it must be from God, but if it was bad then I thought it was from the devil. I felt that God was trying to reach me with important messages, so I tried to open myself up more to God by meditating and opening my mind to what He wanted to tell me. I thought that if I could develop my mind, I would be able to reach God. I had been taught that God answers prayers, so I thought that contact with God was just like all other supernatural experiences. I believed that God had given us certain powers that we did not use anymore, but that they could be developed. I figured that I didn't need the Bible, all I needed was to meditate.

One day I watched a TV program about people who could make things move without touching them, travel through time in their mind, or communicate with the supernatural world. This inspired me to look into the supernatural more seriously. I decided I would visit places where people had died and go out at night looking for UFO's where people had reported seeing them.

In my last year of high school I heard a story of a girl who had died when she fell off her horse at midnight in the mountains. It was said that once a month the girl came back to where she had died. My sister and I rented an old two-story ranch house not too far from where the accident happened. The house had three bedrooms upstairs and four bedrooms downstairs. We let other people stay in some of the bedrooms downstairs, but I had the whole upstairs to myself. Everyone else was afraid to stay in the upstairs bedrooms because noises were heard coming from them at different times in the night. My bedroom was the first room at the top of the stairs. I could see anyone who came up or down the stairs.

One night after I came home from searching for this dead girl, or ghost, I went to my room as usual. It was dark, but there was a light on in the hallway. I could see if anyone was coming up or going down the stairs, but they couldn't see me. As I was looking at the stairs from my bed, I saw the form of a girl coming up the stairs. She passed my room. I waited for her to go back down the stairs, but she never did. When I checked with the others downstairs, I found out that they had heard footsteps, then a woman screaming outside, but there was no one there. I did not go looking for ghosts after that experience. I realized that if you really wanted a dead person, or demon, to visit you, you could make it happen.

My sister also dabbled in the supernatural. She had a board game that if you touched it in a certain spot, it would spell out the answer to your question. I asked her if I could use it. I wanted to see where its power came from, so I asked it. It spelled out H-e-y-l-e-l, which is the Hebrew word for the devil or Lucifer. It gave me a bad feeling, so I told her not to use it anymore.

One evening I drove my girlfriend and her mother to our home. As soon as I shut the car off in the driveway, it burst into flames. The whole front end was on fire. There were flames coming up from the floor and from the sides of the front doors. I jumped out through the flames, and my girlfriend's mother jumped out of her door. As I looked back at the car, I noticed my girlfriend was still in the car. I went back to get her out. I reached in to get her. The flames covered my left arm and side, but my girlfriend and I never got burned, not even our hair. There was a Power watching over us. I ran into the house and told everyone to get out because I thought the car might blow up. If it did blow up, I figured it would take the house with it. We immediately called the fire department, and they arrived quickly and put out the fire. Everyone was okay, but the car was totaled.

The next day my sister told me she was sorry about the fire. She then explained how she and some friends were having a séance, and just before I drove up, the medium screamed and ran out into the orchard. My sisters and her friends follow him, and they saw something that looked like half man, half beast come out from behind a tree and start choking the medium. She said they ran toward the medium and dragged him back into the house just when I drove up and then my car burst into flames. Needless to say, my sister never had a séance again.

Although this scared me, I kept meditating and trying to develop my mind to use what I thought was God-given powers. Next, I began experimenting with astral projection, which is a phenomenon where you can leave your body and go other places. Also, I began practicing moving things with my mind. Once while I was driving, I honked my horn at a friend without even touching it, which I thought was really cool. Another time a friend in prison called to me three times through astral projection. Years later he told me about that night, and I remembered hearing someone calling my name three times, but when I looked no one was there.

I continued playing around with astral projection, mind control, and communicating with the spirits. I believed they were all God-given abilities to use for good, and I thought I was in control of these so-called powers. One night while I was experimenting with astral projection and leaving my body, something felt different. I felt like my mind was being taken from me, and I had no control. I felt as if my mind was going into space and the stars were passing me at hundreds of miles an hour. I couldn't stop it, and I felt as if I was never coming back. Something or some power was in control. In a brief moment of consciousness, I wondered if God was trying to tell me something, and if so, why I was so afraid. Could it be Satan trying to take my mind? One thing I knew for sure, I had no control to stop it. I cried out to God three times to save me, and it all stopped.

God saved my life that night from the powers of darkness. For the first time in my life, I had an overwhelming desire to read the Bible for myself. I wanted to know this God who had saved my life so many times and who had sent His angels to be with me. For years God had tried to reach me, but it wasn't until I opened His Word that I found peace. For all the questions I had, the Bible held the answers. I prayed that God would take all these supernatural powers away if they were not from Him and that I would not see or be harassed by anymore ghosts, demons, or spirit beings. God instantly took all of these things out of my life, although I did have one final supernatural encounter that I will share later on in the book.

Chapter 2

God's Love for Me

As I read God's Word I learned how much God loved me. I read John 3:16, 17: "For God so loved the world, that he gave his only begotten Son, that whosoever believeth in him should not perish, but have everlasting life. For God sent not his Son into the world to condemn the world; but that the world through him might be saved." I let the words sink in—God sent His Son to save me. I just needed to believe, which I did, for I recognize that God had saved my life so many times. There was so much I didn't understand, but I quickly embraced the truth that God and Jesus loved me.

I had never heard of Jesus' death for my sins, but now I discovered the truth about God's love for us and His directive for us to love others: "Beloved, let us love one another: for love is of God; and every one that loveth is born of God, and knoweth God. He that loveth not knoweth not God; for God is love. In this was manifested the love of God toward us, because that God sent his only begotten Son into the world, that we might live through him. Herein is love, not that we loved God, but that he loved us, and sent his Son to be the propitiation for our sins" (1 John 4:7–10). I also read that " the wages of sin is death; but the gift of God is eternal life through Jesus Christ our Lord" (Rom. 6:23).

I learned that eternal life is a gift from God in Christ and that before I even came to Christ He had already paid the price. Paul wrote, "For when we were yet without strength, in due time Christ died for the ungodly. For scarcely for a righteous man will one die: yet peradventure for a good man some would even dare to die. But God commendeth his love toward us, in that, while we were yet sinners, Christ died for us. Much more then, being now justified by his blood, we shall be saved from wrath through him. For if, when we were enemies, we were reconciled to God by the death of his Son, much more, being reconciled, we shall be saved by his life" (Rom. 5:6–10). I marveled at the fact that we have been reconciled to God through Christ: "Even the righteousness of God which is by faith of Jesus Christ unto all and upon all them that believe: for there is no difference: for all have sinned, and come short of the glory of God" (Rom. 3:22, 23).

> "For God so loved the world, that he gave his only begotten Son..."

As I read about how much God loves us, I wanted to change my life. I chose to believe in God and His love. Romans 2:4—"Or despisest thou the riches of his goodness and forbearance and longsuffering; not knowing that the goodness of God leadeth thee to repentance?"—says that the goodness of God leads us to repentance.

That is exactly what happened in my life. I praise God that He doesn't want anyone to be lost: "The Lord is not slack concerning his promise, as some men count slackness; but is longsuffering to us-ward, not willing that any should perish, but that all should come to repentance" (2 Peter 3:9).

After reading about God's love, I discovered that He is preparing a place for us in heaven. John 14:1–6 thrilled my soul: "Let not your heart be troubled: ye believe in God, believe also in me. In my Father's house are many mansions: if it were not so, I would have told you. I go to prepare a place for you. And if I go and prepare a place for you, I will come again, and receive you unto myself; that where I am, there ye may be also. And whither I go ye know, and the way ye know. Thomas saith unto him, Lord, we know not whither thou goest; and how can we know the way? Jesus saith unto him, I am the way, the truth, and the life: no man cometh unto the Father, but by me."

As I studied the Scriptures, I learned about my Lord and Savior (John 5:39). "For this is good and acceptable in the sight of God our Saviour; who will have all men to be saved, and to come unto the knowledge of the truth. For there is one God, and one mediator between God and men, the man Christ Jesus; who gave himself a ransom for all, to be testified in due time" (1 Tim. 2:3–6). God desires all to be saved and to come to the knowledge of the truth through study of the Scripture, which gives us instruction on how we should live that we may be complete for every good work (2 Tim. 3:16, 17).

"Now all these things happened unto them for examples: and they are written for our admonition, upon whom the ends of the world are come" (1 Cor. 10:11).

The Bible is full of examples to prepare us for what is to come. As I studied, I came across this text in Isaiah that tells us how to study: "Whom shall he teach knowledge? and whom shall he make to understand doctrine? them that are weaned from the milk, and drawn from the breasts. For precept must be upon precept, precept upon precept; line upon line, line upon line; here a little and there a little" (Isa. 28:9, 10).

I determined that I should choose a subject of study and find all the verses pertaining to that subject and compare verse with verse. I found that if there was a contradiction in the Bible it was because I was adding my own interpretation. I decided that if I came to the wrong understanding it was because of my preconceived ideas, which I needed to put away in order to accept the Bible just as it is.

> We have also a more sure word of prophecy; whereunto ye do well that ye take heed, as unto a light that shineth in a dark place, until the day dawn, and the day star arise in your hearts: Knowing this first, that no prophecy of the scripture is of any private interpretation. For the prophecy came not in old time by the will of man: but holy men of God spake as they were moved by the Holy Ghost. (2 Peter 1:19–21)

I quickly learned that God loved me and that Christ was my Savior, but He had so many other things He wanted to teach me from His Word. I discovered that all of the questions I had could be answered in God's Word. What a refreshing new revelation!

Chapter 3

State of the Dead

As I studied, I wondered about all the ghosts or spirits of dead people I had seen. I was learning that God is love, but something did not make sense to me. How could a loving God torture people by making them burn in hell forever? And what about the people who supposedly went to heaven? How could they be happy watching all the pain and suffering of their families here on earth? I dug deeper into the Bible to find answers to these questions.

In John 14 I found this promise:

> And I will pray the Father, and he shall give you another Comforter, that he may abide with you for ever; even the Spirit of truth; whom the world cannot receive, because it seeth him not, neither knoweth him: but ye know him; for he dwelleth with you, and shall be in you. I will not leave you comfortless: I will come to you.... But the Comforter, which is the Holy Ghost, whom the Father

> will send in my name, he shall teach you all things, and bring all things to your remembrance, whatsoever I have said unto you. (John 14:16–18, 26)

So I prayed and asked God to guide me and give me answers. In answer to my prayer, the Holy Spirit guided me to the following tests: "For the living know that they shall die: but the dead know not any thing, neither have they any more a reward; for the memory of them is forgotten. Also their love, and their hatred, and their envy, is now perished; neither have they any more a portion for ever in any thing that is done under the sun" (Eccles. 9:5, 6); "For in death there is no remembrance of thee: in the grave who shall give thee thanks?" (Ps. 6:5); "The dead praise not the Lord, neither any that go down into silence" (Ps. 115:17). This was definitely news to me, which led me to further questions.

Where do people go when they die? I then came across the story of Lazarus, which provided another piece to the puzzle in regards to death: "These things said he: and after that he saith unto them, Our friend Lazarus sleepeth; but I go, that I may awake him out of sleep. Then said his disciples, Lord, if he sleep, he shall do well. Howbeit Jesus spake of his death: but they thought that he had spoken of taking of rest in sleep. Then said Jesus unto them plainly, Lazarus is dead" (John 11:11–14).

Jesus compared death to a sleep. And I discovered that the Bible compares death to a sleep more than fifty times. My next question was that if the dead are asleep, when do they wake up from death? The story of Lazarus provided that answer as well.

> Then said Martha unto Jesus, Lord, if thou hadst been here, my brother had not died. But I know, that even now, whatsoever thou wilt ask of God, God will give it thee. Jesus saith unto her, Thy brother shall rise again. Martha saith unto him, I know that he shall rise again in the resurrection at the last day. Jesus said unto her, I am the resurrection, and the life: he that believeth in me, though he were dead, yet shall he live. (John 11:21–25)

Martha said her brother would rise again in the resurrection at the last day. Then Jesus said, "I am the resurrection." According to this verse, I figured out that the dead wake up when Jesus comes back. Paul also talked about rising again: "I have fought a good fight, I have finished my course, I have kept the faith: Henceforth there is laid up for me a crown of righteousness, which the Lord, the righteous judge, shall give me at that day: and not to me only, but unto all them also that love his appearing" (2 Tim. 4:7, 8). And even before that, Job talked about it in the Old Testament: "For I know that my redeemer liveth, and that he shall stand at the latter day upon the earth: And though after my skin worms destroy this body, yet in my flesh shall I see God: Whom I shall see for myself, and mine eyes shall behold, and not another; though my reins be consumed within me" (Job 19:25–27).

I learned that the Bible talks about two resurrections. "Marvel not at this: for the hour is coming, in the which all that are in the graves shall hear his voice, and shall come forth; they that have done good, unto the resurrection of life; and they that have done evil, unto the resurrection of damnation" (John 5:28, 29). The first resurrection is when Christ comes for His people: "For the Lord himself shall descend from heaven with a shout, with the voice of the archangel, and with the trump of God: and the dead in Christ shall rise first: Then we which are alive and remain shall be caught up together with them in the clouds, to meet the Lord in the air: and so shall we ever be with the Lord. Wherefore comfort one another with these words" (1 Thess. 4:16–18).

I got excited as I thought about becoming immortal.

> Behold, I shew you a mystery; We shall not all sleep, but we shall all be changed, In a moment, in the twinkling of an eye, at the last trump: for the trumpet shall sound, and the dead shall be raised incorruptible, and we shall be changed. For this corruptible must put on incorruption, and this mortal must put on immortality. So when this corruptible shall have put on incorruption, and this mortal shall have put on immortality, then shall be brought to pass the saying that is written, Death is swallowed up in victory. O death, where is thy sting? O grave, where is thy victory?" (1 Cor. 15:51–55).

I realized that we cannot have immortality on this earth and that anything that gives this portrayal is of Satan.

As I read Genesis, I learned about the first sin, and the first death sentence. God told Adam in the Garden of Eden that if he ate from the tree of the knowledge of good and evil he would die. "And the Lord God commanded the man, saying, Of every tree of the garden thou mayest freely eat: But of the tree of the knowledge of good and evil, thou shalt not eat of it: for in the day that thou eatest thereof thou shalt surely die" (Gen. 2:16, 17). Satan lied to Eve and told her that she wouldn't die if she ate the fruit (Gen. 3:4). It hit me that I was no better than Eve. I had been tricked by Satan and had listened to his lies that toying with the dark side wouldn't hurt me. I had also believed his falsehoods about heaven and hell and death. Now I was learning the truth, the truth that you sleep in the grave until the resurrection day and the only thing that returns to God is His breath of life (Gen. 2:7; Job 27:3–5; Ps. 146:4).

After learning about the first resurrection of the righteous, I studied my Bible to find out what happened to the wicked. "Marvel not at this: for the hour is coming, in the which all that are in the graves shall hear his voice, and shall come forth; they that have done good, unto the resurrection of life; and they that have done evil, unto the resurrection of damnation" (John 5:28, 29). According to this verse, there will be two resurrections. When Christ comes back, according to 1 Thessalonians 4:16, 17, He sends His angels to gather His followers. It's clear from this verse that all God's people will meet the Lord in the air: the righteous living and the righteous dead. This is the first resurrection.

At Christ's second coming all the wicked will be destroyed. They will not be able to look upon Christ. They will be destroyed by the brightness of His coming. God gave them every chance to be saved, but they rejected the Word of God and are lost by their own choice.

> And the heaven departed as a scroll when it is rolled together; and every mountain and island were moved out of their places. And the kings of the earth, and the great men, and the rich men, and the chief captains, and the mighty men, and every bondman, and every free man, hid themselves in the dens and in the rocks of the mountains; and said to the mountains and rocks, Fall on us, and hide us from the face of him that sitteth on the throne, and from the wrath of the Lamb: For the great day of his wrath is come; and who shall be able to stand? (Rev 6:14–17)

I excitedly continued studying, and I found out that there is a thousand years between the two resurrections.

> And I saw thrones, and they sat upon them, and judgment was given unto them: and I saw the souls of them that were beheaded for the witness of Jesus, and for the word of God, and which had not worshipped the beast, neither his image, neither had received his mark upon their foreheads, or in their hands; and they lived and reigned with Christ a thousand years. But the rest of the dead lived not again until the thousand years were finished. This is the first resurrection. Blessed and holy is he that hath part in the first resurrection: on such the second death hath no power, but they shall be priests of God and of Christ, and shall reign with him a thousand years. (Rev. 20:4–6)

During the thousand years, the wicked are in their graves and Satan is bound to this earth. The righteous who were raised at the first resurrection are in heaven reviewing the books. At this time we will be allowed to ask Jesus questions about the judgment and who is there and who isn't. I know I will have plenty of questions about the supernatural things that happened in my life, why certain people in my life had to die so young, and why this person is in heaven and this other person is not. I can't wait to talk to Jesus face to face and have all of life's questions answered once and for all.

As I studied about the resurrection, I came to the part about the destruction of the wicked, and I gained a true understanding of hell based on Revelation 20:7–9:

> And when the thousand years are expired, Satan shall be loosed out of his prison, and shall go out to deceive the nations which are in the four quarters of the earth, Gog, and Magog, to gather them together to battle: the number of whom is as the sand of the sea. And they went up on the breadth of the earth, and compassed the camp of the saints about, and the beloved city: and fire came down from God out of heaven, and devoured them.

According to these verses, Satan and his followers surround the beloved city on earth and prepare for battle. Then God sends fire down out of heaven and destroys them. I found additional insight into the destruction of the wicked in verses 12–15:

> And I saw the dead, small and great, stand before God; and the books were opened: and another book was opened, which is the book of life: and the dead were judged out of those things which were written in the books, according to their works. And the sea gave up the dead which were in it; and death and hell delivered up the dead which were in them: and they were judged every man according to their works. And death and hell were cast into the lake of fire. This is the second death. And whosoever was not found written in the book of life was cast into the lake of fire."

Thus, the Bible teaches that all the wicked will be cast into the lake of fire. I was relieved to realize that the loving God I was learning about does not want to torture the wicked forever. Even though Revelation 20:10 states that "the devil that deceived them was cast into the lake of fire and brimstone, where the beast and the false prophet are, and shall be tormented day and night for ever and ever," verse 9 already clarified that "fire came down from God out of heaven, and devoured them." Someone that is "devoured" is not burning forever.

> Seeing it is a righteous thing with God to recompense tribulation to them that trouble you; and to you who are troubled rest with us, when the Lord Jesus shall be revealed from heaven with his mighty angels, in flaming fire taking vengeance on them that know not God, and that obey not the gospel of our Lord Jesus Christ: who shall be punished

> with everlasting destruction from the presence of the Lord, and from the glory of his power. (2 Thess. 1:6–9)

Paul made it clear in this passage that the wicked will be destroyed with everlasting destruction; they will not burn forever and ever. Another verse that helped me understand this is Jude 1:7: "Even as Sodom and Gomorrha, and the cities about them in like manner, giving themselves over to fornication, and going after strange flesh, are set forth for an example, suffering the vengeance of eternal fire." The destruction of Sodom and Gomorrha are an example of eternal fire. They were burned up and utterly destroyed, but they are not still burning.

The wicked will be completely destroyed and reduced to ashes under our feet. Even Satan himself will be reduced to ashes. But no one will burn forever.

> For, behold, the day cometh, that shall burn as an oven; and all the proud, yea, and all that do wickedly, shall be stubble: and the day that cometh shall burn them up, saith the LORD of hosts, that it shall leave them neither root nor branch. But unto you that fear my name shall the Sun of righteousness arise with healing in his wings; and ye shall go forth, and grow up as calves of the stall. And ye shall tread down the wicked; for they shall be ashes under the soles of your feet in the day that I shall do this, saith the LORD of hosts. (Mal. 4:1–3).

> Thine heart was lifted up because of thy beauty, thou hast corrupted thy wisdom by reason of thy brightness: I will cast thee to the ground, I will lay thee before kings, that they may behold thee. Thou hast defiled thy sanctuaries by the multitude of thine iniquities, by the iniquity of thy traffick; therefore will I bring forth a fire from the midst of thee, it shall devour thee, and I will bring thee to ashes upon the earth in the sight of all them that behold thee. All they that know thee among the people shall be astonished at thee: thou shalt be a terror, and never shalt thou be any more. (Ezek. 28:17–19)

We don't know how long hell fire will burn, but it will burn until all the wicked are devoured. Then God will wipe away our tears.

> And God shall wipe away all tears from their eyes; and there shall be no more death, neither sorrow, nor crying, neither shall there be any more pain: for the former things are passed away. And he that sat upon the throne said, Behold, I make all things new. And he said unto me, Write: for these words are true and faithful. And he said unto me, It is done. I am Alpha and Omega, the beginning and the end. I will give unto him that is athirst of the fountain of the water of life freely. He that overcometh shall inherit all things; and I will be his God, and he shall be my son. (Rev 21:4–7)

I praised God for the marvelous new things I was learning and the promise that all who are overcomers in Christ shall inherit the new earth. What an exciting thought!

Chapter 4

Satan Has Counterfeits

Upon learning the truth about death, I came to the conclusion that for every truth in God's Word Satan has a counterfeit message to deceive people. God says that when you die you sleep until the resurrection day; Satan says that you live forever, bad or good. Christ says when He comes back every eye will see Him (Rev. 1:7); Satan says it will be a secret. God blessed the seventh-day Sabbath of the fourth commandment and asked us to keep it holy; Satan says we should keep the first day of the week, Sunday, as the Sabbath.

The more I studied, the more I discovered that Satan mixes truth with lies. Satan and His ministers perform miracles, signs, and lying wonders to deceive people. Satan deceived me because I didn't know anything about the Word of God. All the supernatural experiences I had were all a deception of Satan, lying wonders mixed with Christianity. What I saw and did was real, but none of it was of God.

I took the counsel of Jeremiah 29:13 seriously—"And ye shall seek me, and find me, when ye shall search for me with all your heart"—and I continued studying. When we search Scripture with all our heart, we will discover the truth (John 17:17), and we will be sanctified when we follow God's voice. "Behold, I stand at the door, and knock: if any man hear my voice, and open the door, I will come in to him, and will sup with him, and he with me. To him that overcometh will I grant to sit with me in my throne, even as I also overcame, and am set down with my Father in his throne" (Rev. 3:20, 21)

> "... for every truth in God's Word Satan has a counterfeit message to deceive people."

Jesus is knocking at the door of your heart as he was at my heart. If you let Him in, you will be an overcomer like Jesus and will be granted the honor of sitting next to Jesus in heaven as is described in Revelation 20:4: "And I saw thrones, and they sat upon them, and judgment was given unto them: and I saw the souls of them that were beheaded for the witness of Jesus, and for the word of God, and which had not worshipped the beast, neither his image, neither had received his mark upon their foreheads, or in their hands; and they lived and reigned with Christ a thousand years."

I grew excited when I read in 2 Peter 1:2–4 about being a partaker of Christ's character: "Grace and peace be multiplied unto you through the knowledge of God, and of Jesus our Lord, According as his divine power hath given unto us all things that pertain unto life and godliness, through the knowledge of him that hath called us to glory and virtue: Whereby are given unto us exceeding great and precious promises: that by these ye might be partakers of the divine nature, having escaped the corruption that is in the world through lust."

Although I hadn't attended church that much growing up, I had heard that Christ would secretly come back a second time. Now, as I studied the Bible, I discovered that Satan had caused me to believe another lie. Revelation 1:7 assures us that every eye will see Him: "Behold, he cometh with clouds; and every eye shall see him, and they also which pierced him: and all kindreds of the earth shall wail because of him. Even so, Amen." That's very clear, Christ is coming in the clouds, and every eye will see Him.

I was grateful to find Christ's warning to His disciples regarding Satan's trickery:

> Then if any man shall say unto you, Lo, here is Christ, or there; believe it not. For there shall arise false Christs, and false prophets, and shall shew great signs and wonders; insomuch that, if it were possible, they shall deceive the very elect. Behold, I have told you before. Wherefore if they shall say unto you, Behold, he is in the desert; go not forth: behold, he is in the secret chambers; believe it not. For as the lightning cometh out of the east, and shineth even unto the west; so shall also the coming of the Son of man be. (Matt 24:23–27)

And then I read 1 Thessalonians 4:16, 17: "For the Lord himself shall descend from heaven with a shout, with the voice of the archangel, and with the trump of God: and the dead in Christ shall rise first: then we which are alive and remain shall be caught up together with them in the clouds, to meet the Lord in the air: and so shall we ever be with the Lord." The Lord is going to shout with the voice of the archangel and the trump of God. Then the dead in Christ shall rise first. The second coming of Jesus is not going to be a quiet event

I came across another verse that talked about the trumpet and the dead rising: "Behold, I shew you a mystery; we shall not all sleep, but we shall all be changed, in a moment, in the twinkling of an eye, at the last trump: for the trumpet shall sound, and the dead shall be raised incorruptible, and we shall be changed" (1 Cor. 15:51, 52). This verse says it again, the trumpet will sound and the dead will be raised incorruptible.

While the righteous rejoice at the coming of the King, the wicked will mourn. "And then shall appear the sign of the Son of man in heaven: and then shall all the tribes of the earth mourn, and they shall see the Son of man coming in the clouds of heaven with power and great glory. And he shall send his angels with a great sound of a trumpet, and they shall gather together his elect from the four winds, from one end of heaven to the other" (Matt 24:30, 31).

We are not in darkness; we are children of the light (1 Thess. 5:2–6). Jesus' coming as a thief is in reference to the unexpected time of Jesus' coming, not the manner of His coming. But to those who are watching for Christ's glorious appearing, we will know when it is close, even at the door.

I had heard people use Matthew 24:40, 41 in defense of a secret rapture, but after reading so many other texts that talked about Christ's return, I felt there had to be another explanation. Then I read Luke 17:26–37:

> And as it was in the days of Noe [Noah], so shall it be also in the days of the Son of man. They did eat, they drank, they married wives, they were given in marriage, until the day that Noe entered into the ark, and the flood came, and destroyed them all.
>
> Likewise also as it was in the days of Lot; they did eat, they drank, they bought, they sold, they planted, they builded; but the same day that Lot went out of Sodom it rained fire and brimstone from heaven, and destroyed them all. Even thus shall it be in the day when the Son of man is revealed. In that day, he which shall be upon the housetop, and his stuff in the house, let him not come down to take it away: and he that is in the field, let him likewise not return back. Remember Lot's wife.
>
> Whosoever shall seek to save his life shall lose it; and whosoever shall lose his life shall preserve it. I tell you, in that night there shall be two men in one bed; the one shall be taken, and the other shall be left. Two women shall be grinding together; the one shall be taken, and the other left. Two men shall be in the field; the one shall be taken, and the other left. And they answered and said unto him, Where, Lord? And he said

> unto them, Wheresoever the body is, thither will the eagles be gathered together.

Verses 26 and 27 describe Noah's day and the two classes of people: the righteous who were saved and the wicked who were destroyed by the flood. When Christ comes again, one class will be taken to heaven and the other class will be destroyed (2 Thess. 1:7–9; 2:8). The more I studied, the more I determined that I wanted to go to heaven to live with Jesus forever (1 Thess. 4:17).

As I accepted these Bible truths, I had a deep desire to share with others what I was learning. I attended many youth and young adult meetings and shared with those in attendance what I was studying. Unfortunately, I soon found out that the leaders of these meetings didn't want me to say anything. They wanted to operate under the premise that Jesus loves you and the details of the Bible, such as how Jesus was coming back, didn't matter. I shared with the group that, yes, Jesus loves them, but as part of loving Him in return, Christ wants to teach us truths and help us to grow through His Word.

I felt strongly that the Bible was a "lamp unto my feet, and a light unto my path" ...

I felt strongly that the Bible was a "lamp unto my feet, and a light unto my path" (Ps. 119:105) and that God's Word would guide me if I hid it in my heart (Ps. 119:11). I was thankful that God had sent the Holy Spirit to guide me into the truth (John 16:13).

The story of Jesus being tempted in the wilderness gave me courage to keep studying and sharing

Scripture, even if others didn't believe, such as the leaders from the youth group, for I knew I was protecting myself against the devil's deceptions.

> Then was Jesus led up of the Spirit into the wilderness to be tempted of the devil. And when he had fasted forty days and forty nights, he was afterward an hungered. And when the tempter came to him, he said, If thou be the Son of God, command that these stones be made bread. But he answered and said, It is written, Man shall not live by bread alone, but by every word that proceedeth out of the mouth of God.
>
> Then the devil taketh him up into the holy city, and setteth him on a pinnacle of the temple, and saith unto him, If thou be the Son of God, cast thyself down: for it is written, He shall give his angels charge concerning thee: and in their hands they shall bear thee up, lest at any time thou dash thy foot against a stone. Jesus said unto him, It is written again, Thou shalt not tempt the Lord thy God.
>
> Again, the devil taketh him up into an exceeding high mountain, and sheweth him all the kingdoms of the world, and the glory of them; and saith unto him, All these things will I give thee, if thou wilt fall down and worship me. Then saith Jesus unto him, Get thee hence, Satan: for it is written, Thou shalt worship the Lord thy God, and him only shalt thou serve. Then the devil leaveth

> him, and, behold, angels came and ministered unto him. (Matt. 4:1–11)

Our only defense from Satan is God's Word. It is written. "Study to shew thyself approved unto God, a workman that needeth not to be ashamed, rightly dividing the word of truth" (2 Tim. 2:15). I continued studying in order to prove all things by God's Word.

Our only defense from Satan is God's Word.

Chapter 5

Falling Away

As time passed, I slowly didn't study as much as I used to. I worked all day at my regular job, and then when I got home, I would work half the night away in my shop. It seemed I was too busy trying to make a living than study God's Word. If Satan can't get you one way, he tries another. Before I knew it I didn't have time to study at all. My prayer time slowly faded away also, and my past came back to haunt me—literally.

One night I went to bed late like I usually did. The rest of the family was already asleep. I had just crawled into bed when I heard a knock at the front door. I got up and went to answer the door. When I opened the door, there was something standing there that looked like half man and half beast. Upon seeing this creature, I lost all my strength and turned and fell to the floor. I still remember it as if it happened yesterday. The creature then put one hand around my throat and picked me up off the floor. It held me by the neck and began choking me! I couldn't do anything to fight back!

As the devil sought to claim my life and steal me away from God, I remembered Christ and His promise to never leave me nor forsake me. I realized that I was the one who had left Him when I didn't have time to study or pray. All I could think of was God's assurance to fear not for He was with me and would give me strength and help me in my time of need—"Fear thou not; for I am with thee" (Isa. 41:10). As I called out to God to deliver me from this demon creature, it released me, and I dropped to the floor. After regaining my strength, I locked the door and headed back to bed, but I couldn't sleep. I prayed the rest of the night and asked God for forgiveness. I knew this was my fault.

Because I had not fully submitted myself to God, I was not able to resist the devil

Because I had not fully submitted myself to God, I was not able to resist the devil (James 4:7, 8). I realized that I needed to take seriously my walk with God and put on the armor of God anew each day:

> Finally, my brethren, be strong in the Lord, and in the power of his might. Put on the whole armour of God, that ye may be able to stand against the wiles of the devil. For we wrestle not against flesh and blood, but against principalities, against powers, against the rulers of the darkness of this world, against spiritual wickedness in high places. Wherefore take unto you the whole armour of God, that ye may be able to

> withstand in the evil day, and having done all, to stand. Stand therefore, having your loins girt about with truth, and having on the breastplate of righteousness; and your feet shod with the preparation of the gospel of peace; above all, taking the shield of faith, wherewith ye shall be able to quench all the fiery darts of the wicked. And take the helmet of salvation, and the sword of the Spirit, which is the word of God: Praying always with all prayer and supplication in the Spirit, and watching thereunto with all perseverance and supplication for all saints. (Eph. 6:10–18)

I learned that it's not a once saved always saved ... We must abide in Christ daily

I recommitted my life to God and determined to make Him first in my life. I learned that it's not a once saved always saved kind of relationship that Christ wanted with me. We must abide in Christ daily (Luke 9:23; 1 Cor. 15:31). I realized I had to daily give my life to Christ. He was not forcing me to follow Him. It was my choice—a choice I needed to make every day.

> I am the vine, ye are the branches: He that abideth in me, and I in him, the same bringeth forth much fruit: for without me ye can do nothing. If a man abide not in me, he is

> cast forth as a branch, and is withered; and men gather them, and cast them into the fire, and they are burned. If ye abide in me, and my words abide in you, ye shall ask what ye will, and it shall be done unto you. Herein is my Father glorified ,that ye bear much fruit; so shall ye be my disciples. (John 15:5–8)

> Now therefore fear the LORD, and serve him in sincerity and in truth: and put away the gods which your fathers served on the other side of the flood, and in Egypt; and serve ye the LORD. And if it seem evil unto you to serve the LORD, choose you this day whom ye will serve; whether the gods which your fathers served that were on the other side of the flood, or the gods of the Amorites, in whose land ye dwell: but as for me and my house, we will serve the Lord. (Joshua 24:14, 15)

It's our choice. As God delivered the children of Israel from Egypt and from their false gods, so God will deliver us out of this world of sin and from the gods of this world. Anything that we put before Christ can become our god. I realized that I was working so hard to earn money that I had pushed God away and was laying up my treasures on earth instead of in heaven.

Anything that we put before Christ can become our god.

> Lay not up for yourselves treasures upon earth, where moth and rust doth corrupt, and

> where thieves break through and steal: But lay up for yourselves treasures in heaven, where neither moth nor rust doth corrupt, and where thieves do not break through nor steal: For where your treasure is, there will your heart be also.... No man can serve two masters: for either he will hate the one, and love the other; or else he will hold to the one, and despise the other. Ye cannot serve God and mammon.... Therefore take no thought, saying, What shall we eat? or, What shall we drink? or, Wherewithal shall we be clothed? (For after all these things do the Gentiles seek:) for your heavenly Father knoweth that ye have need of all these things. But seek ye first the kingdom of God, and his righteousness; and all these things shall be added unto you. Take therefore no thought for the morrow: for the morrow shall take thought for the things of itself. Sufficient unto the day is the evil thereof. (Matt. 6:19–34)

Christ's words are so beautiful and powerful. Christ knows our every need, but He asks us to seek His kingdom and righteousness first. And we do that by reading the Bible, not as a regular book, but with the revelation that God is speaking to you through each page.

I made a new commitment to God to pray and study His word every day. There was so much more I still needed to learn. I understood that God loved me and was calling me to be a part of His family, but the Bible was full of living truths I needed to grasp.

> Blessed be the God and Father of our Lord Jesus Christ, who hath blessed us with all spiritual blessings in heavenly places in Christ: According as he hath chosen us in him before the foundation of the world, that we should be holy and without blame before him in love: Having predestinated us unto the adoption of children by Jesus Christ to himself, according to the good pleasure of his will, to the praise of the glory of his grace, wherein he hath made us accepted in the beloved. In whom we have redemption through his blood, the forgiveness of sins, according to the riches of his grace. (Eph. 1:3–7)

For as many as are led by the Spirit of God, they are the sons of God. For ye have not received the spirit of bondage again to fear; but ye have received the Spirit of adoption, whereby we cry, Abba, Father. (Rom. 8:14, 15)

Chapter 6

Growing in Christ

I marveled at God's desire to adopt us back into His family and His promise to write His law on our hearts. I was convicted again of God's love, and in response, I wanted to keep His commandments and honor Him in this way. The following verses were a blessing to me as I renewed my commitment to God.

> This is the covenant that I will make with them after those days, saith the Lord, I will put my laws into their hearts, and in their minds will I write them; and their sins and iniquities will I remember no more. (Heb. 10:16)

> If ye love me, keep my commandments.... He that hath my commandments, and keepeth them, he it is that loveth me: and he that loveth me shall be loved of my Father, and I will love him, and will manifest myself to him. (John 14:15, 21)

> As the Father hath loved me, so have I loved you: continue ye in my love. If ye keep my commandments, ye shall abide in my love; even as I have kept my Father's commandments, and abide in his love. (John 15:9, 10)

> Praise ye the LORD. Blessed is the man that feareth the LORD, that delighteth greatly in his commandments. (Ps. 112:1)

> Let us hear the conclusion of the whole matter: Fear God, and keep his commandments: for this is the whole duty of man. For God shall bring every work into judgment, with every secret thing, whether it be good, or whether it be evil. (Eccles. 12:13, 14)

> Here is the patience of the saints: here are they that keep the commandments of God, and the faith of Jesus. (Rev. 14:12)

> Blessed are they that do his commandments, that they may have right to the tree of life, and may enter in through the gates into the city. (Rev. 22:14)

I took comfort in knowing that, through the power of the Holy Spirit, I could overcome sin in my life by following Christ's example of how to live. I also took comfort in knowing that if I stumbled and fell at times Jesus was my advocate in heaven and would help me get back on the right path.

Behold, what manner of love the Father hath bestowed upon us, that we should be called the sons of God: therefore the world knoweth us not, because it knew him not. Beloved, now are we the sons of God, and it doth not yet appear what we shall be: but we know that, when he shall appear, we shall be like him; for we shall see him as he is. And every man that hath this hope in him purifieth himself, even as he is pure. Whosoever committeth sin transgresseth also the law: for sin is the transgression of the law. And ye know that he was manifested to take away our sins; and in him is no sin. Whosoever abideth in him sinneth not: whosoever sinneth hath not seen him, neither known him. Little children, let no man deceive you: he that doeth righteousness is righteous, even as he is righteous. He that committeth sin is of the devil; for the devil sinneth from the beginning. For this purpose the Son of God was manifested, that he might destroy the works of the devil. Whosoever is born of God doth not commit sin; for his seed remaineth in him: and he cannot sin, because he is born of God.... And he that keepeth his commandments dwelleth in him, and he in him. And hereby we know that he abideth in us, by the Spirit which he hath given us. (1 John 3:1–9, 24)

But if we walk in the light, as he is in the light, we have fellowship one with another,

> and the blood of Jesus Christ his Son cleanseth us from all sin. If we say that we have no sin, we deceive ourselves, and the truth is not in us. If we confess our sins, he is faithful and just to forgive us our sins, and to cleanse us from all unrighteousness. (1 John 1:7–9)

> My little children, these things write I unto you, that ye sin not. And if any man sin, we have an advocate with the Father, Jesus Christ the righteous: And he is the propitiation for our sins: and not for ours only, but also for the sins of the whole world. And hereby we do know that we know him, if we keep his commandments. He that saith, I know him, and keepeth not his commandments, is a liar, and the truth is not in him. But whoso keepeth his word, in him verily is the love of God perfected: hereby know we that we are in him. He that saith he abideth in him ought himself also so to walk, even as he walked. (1 John 2:1–6)

> Knowing this, that our old man is crucified with him, that the body of sin might be destroyed, that henceforth we should not serve sin.... Let not sin therefore reign in your mortal body, that ye should obey it in the lusts thereof. (Rom. 6:6, 12)

As I read about the importance of keeping God's law, I turned to Exodus 20 and read the Ten Commandments with a fresh eye. As I read I saw that the first four commandments speak to our love for God and the last six deal with our relationship with others.

> Thou shalt have no other gods before me.
>
> Thou shalt not make unto thee any graven image, or any likeness of any thing that is in heaven above, or that is in the earth beneath, or that is in the water under the earth: Thou shalt not bow down thyself to them, nor serve them: for I the LORD thy God am a jealous God, visiting the iniquity of the fathers upon the children unto the third and fourth generation of them that hate me; And shewing mercy unto thousands of them that love me, and keep my commandments.
>
> Thou shalt not take the name of the LORD thy God in vain; for the LORD will not hold him guiltless that taketh his name in vain.
>
> Remember the sabbath day, to keep it holy. Six days shalt thou labour, and do all thy work: But the seventh day is the sabbath of the LORD thy God: in it thou shalt not do any work, thou, nor thy son, nor thy daughter, thy manservant, nor thy maidservant, nor thy cattle, nor thy stranger that is within thy gates: For in six days the LORD made heaven and earth, the sea, and all that in them is, and rested the seventh day: wherefore the LORD blessed the sabbath day, and hallowed it.
>
> Honour thy father and thy mother: that thy days may be long upon the land which the LORD thy God giveth thee.

> Thou shalt not kill.
>
> Thou shalt not commit adultery.
>
> Thou shalt not steal.
>
> Thou shalt not bear false witness against thy neighbour.
>
> Thou shalt not covet thy neighbour's house, thou shalt not covet they neighbour's wife, nor his manservant, nor his maidservant, nor his ox, nor his ass, nor any thing that is thy neighbour's. (Exod. 20:3–17)

Of special interest to me as I read was the fourth commandment. It said to remember the seventh-day Sabbath. I had never thought about which day I worshipped on. I had always gone to church on the first day of the week, Sunday. It was just what we did. But why did this commandment say remember? Could it be that God had given this commandment before writing the Ten Commandments? I found out that He did in Genesis 2:1–3:

> Thus the heavens and the earth were finished, and all the host of them. And on the seventh day God ended his work which he had made; and he rested on the seventh day from all his work which he had made. And God blessed the seventh day, and sanctified it: because that in it he had rested from all his work which God created and made.

The seventh day is the day that God rested on after creating the world. Thus, it was instituted at Creation. I found the Sabbath again in Revelation 14:7: "Saying with a loud voice, Fear God, and give glory to him; for the hour of his judgment is come: and worship him that made heaven, and earth, and the sea, and the fountains of waters." Notice what it says: "Worship him that made heaven, and earth, and the sea, and the fountains of waters." The fourth commandment tells us who created us. It's God's seal. By keeping the seventh-day Sabbath we honor our God and our Creator. "It is a sign between me and the children of Israel for ever: for in six days the LORD made heaven and earth, and on the seventh day he rested, and was refreshed. And he gave unto Moses, when he had made an end of communing with him upon mount Sinai, two tables of testimony, tables of stone, written with the finger of God" (Exod. 31:17, 18).

I discovered that Isaiah called the Sabbath a delight: "If thou turn away thy foot from the sabbath, from doing thy pleasure on my holy day; and call the sabbath a delight, the holy of the LORD, honourable; and shalt honour him, not doing thine own ways, nor finding thine own pleasure, nor speaking thine own words: Then shalt thou delight thyself in the LORD; and I will cause thee to ride upon the high places of the earth, and feed thee with the heritage of Jacob thy father: for the mouth of the LORD hath spoken it" (Isa. 58:13, 14).

By keeping the seventh-day Sabbath we honor our God and our Creator.

I also learned that those who go to heaven will celebrate the Sabbath in the new earth. "For as the new heavens and the new earth, which I will make, shall remain before me, saith the LORD, so shall your seed and your name remain. And it shall come to pass, that from one new moon to another, and from one Sabbath to another, shall all flesh come to worship before me, saith the LORD" (Isa. 66:22, 23).

The more I studied the more I found mention of the Sabbath throughout the Bible. Here are a few verses from the New Testament giving reference as to how Christ and His apostles kept the Sabbath.

> And came down to Capernaum, a city of Galilee, and taught them on the sabbath days. And they were astonished at his doctrine: for his word was with power. (Luke 4:31, 32) "
>
> And he said unto them, That the Son of man is Lord also of the sabbath. And it came to pass also on another sabbath, that he entered into the synagogue and taught: and there was a man whose right hand was withered. (Luke 6:5, 6)
>
> For they that dwell at Jerusalem, and their rulers, because they knew him not, nor yet the voices of the prophets which are read every sabbath day, they have fulfilled them in condemning him. (Acts 13:27)
>
> For Moses of old time hath in every city them that preach him, being read in the synagogues every sabbath day. (Acts 15:21).

The Sabbath is so important that Christ rested in the tomb on the Sabbath day. In Matthew 27 and 28 I read the story of Jesus' burial and was astonished at God's perfect plan, which involved the preparation of Jesus' body before Sabbath.

> He [Joseph of Arimathea] went to Pilate, and begged the body of Jesus. Then Pilate commanded the body to be delivered. And when Joseph had taken the body, he wrapped it in a clean linen cloth, and laid it in his own new tomb, which he had hewn out in the rock: and he rolled a great stone to the door of the sepulchre, and departed. And there was Mary Magdalene, and the other Mary, sitting over against the sepulchre.
>
> Now the next day, that followed the day of the preparation, the chief priests and Pharisees came together unto Pilate, Saying, Sir, we remember that that deceiver said, while he was yet alive, After three days I will rise again. Command therefore that the sepulchre be made sure until the third day, lest his disciples come by night, and steal him away, and say unto the people, He is risen from the dead: so the last error shall be worse than the first. Pilate said unto them, Ye have a watch: go your way, make it as sure as ye can. So they went, and made the sepulchre sure, sealing the stone, and setting a watch.
>
> In the end of the sabbath, as it began to dawn toward the first day of the week, came Mary Magdalene and the other Mary to see the sepulcher. And, behold, there was a great earthquake: for the angel of the Lord

descended from heaven, and came and rolled back the stone from the door, and sat upon it. His countenance was like lightning, and his raiment white as snow: And for fear of him the keepers did shake, and became as dead men. And the angel answered and said unto the women, Fear not ye: for I know that ye seek Jesus, which was crucified. He is not here: for he is risen, as he said. Come, see the place where the Lord lay." (Matt. 27:58–28:6)

And after this Joseph of Arimathaea, being a disciple of Jesus, but secretly for fear of the Jews, besought Pilate that he might take away the body of Jesus: and Pilate gave him leave. He came therefore, and took the body of Jesus. And there came also Nicodemus, which at the first came to Jesus by night, and brought a mixture of myrrh and aloes, about an hundred pound weight. Then took they the body of Jesus, and wound it in linen clothes with the spices, as the manner of the Jews is to bury. Now in the place where he was crucified there was a garden; and in the garden a new sepulchre, wherein was never man yet laid. There laid they Jesus therefore because of the Jews' preparation day; for the sepulchre was nigh at hand. The first day of the week cometh Mary Magdalene early, when it was yet dark, unto the sepulchre, and seeth the stone taken away from the sepulchre. (John 19:38–20:1)

It was so clear to me that the seventh day of the week, Saturday, is the Sabbath ordained at the beginning of Creation. I looked it up in the dictionary and encyclopedia to confirm that Saturday was the seventh day of the week, and they both agreed. I even asked my mom, and she said Saturday was the seventh day. I just couldn't get over why we had always kept Sunday, the first day of the week, as the Sabbath. After making this discovery, my next question was, why do so many other people worship on Sunday?

Why do so many other people worship on Sunday?

I began to ask pastors and church members of various denominations if the Ten Commandments are still binding and if God wants us to live by them. They all said yes. I then asked them about the seventh-day Sabbath in the fourth commandment, and I was told, "Well, it has been changed to the first day of the week, Sunday, in honor of Christ's resurrection."

This drove me to study even more, and I learned that after Christ's death His followers still kept the Sabbath. It seemed to me that if Christ had changed the Sabbath it would be recorded in the New Testament by His apostles. But no where in the Bible could I find that the Sabbath was changed. In fact, I found the following verses that state that Jesus' words do not change: "Jesus Christ the same yesterday, and to day, and for ever" (Heb. 13:8); "My covenant will I not break, nor alter the thing that is gone out of my lips" (Ps. 89:34).

I came to the conclusion that God blessed and sanctified the Sabbath day at Creation (Gen. 2:1–3), and we cannot change that. However, it was clear that although we, as humans, didn't have the right to change the day, someone did, so I kept studying. This led me into the area of prophecy and the book of Daniel where I found that someone would "speak great words against the most High, and shall wear out the saints of the most High, and think to change times and laws: and they shall be given into his hand until a time and times and the dividing of time" (Dan. 7:25). I was fascinated by this prophecy and the other things I was learning in Daniel. I continued reading, trying to determine what church would have, or claim to have, the power to change God's Word, cast truth to the ground, and teach false doctrines.

My girlfriend at the time went to a Catholic Church, so I pulled out a copy of the Catholic catechism to compare it to the Bible. To my surprise, I found that the Catholic Church had changed the Ten Commandments. The church made the first and second commandments one and moved the other commandments up one, which made the Sabbath commandment the third commandment. Then, they split the tenth commandment in two in order to have a total of ten commandments. They also changed the wording of the fourth commandment to read, "Remember to keep holy the Lord's Day." They don't say anything about the seventh-day Sabbath or that God made the world in six days and blessed and sanctified the seventh day.

I couldn't believe my discovery. I felt strongly that the Catholic Church had changed the seventh-day Sabbath from Saturday to Sunday. It was just what Daniel 7:25 talked about. The beast power would "think to change times and laws." But the Bible taught me that you cannot change God's times and laws. They were written by God with His own finger and are unchangeable and perfect.

Through more research I found that the Catholic Church does not even deny that they changed the seventh-day Sabbath to Sunday, the first day of the week. Instead they boldly boast about it. Look at the following statements taken from their own writings:

> Sunday is a Catholic institution and its claim to observance can be defended only on Catholic principles.... From beginning to end of Scripture there is not a single passage that warrants the transfer of weekly public worship from the last day of the week to the first. (*Catholic Press*, Sydney, Australia, August 1900)

> Sunday is our mark of authority ... The church is above the Bible, and this transference of Sabbath observance is proof of that fact. (*The Catholic Record*, London, Ontario, September 1, 1923)

> "Question: Which is the Sabbath day?
> "Answer: Saturday is the Sabbath day.
> "Question: Why do we observe Sunday instead of Saturday?
> "Answer: We observe Sunday instead of Saturday because the Catholic Church in the Council of Laodicea [AD 336] transferred the solemnity from Saturday to Sunday." (Peter Giermann, *Convert's Catechism of Catholic Doctrine*, p. 50)

> Perhaps the boldest thing, the most revolutionary change the Church ever did, happened in the first century [actually it happened in the fourth century]. The holy day, the Sabbath, was changed from Saturday to Sunday. "The Day of the Lord" (dies Dominia) was chosen, not from any directions noted in the Scriptures, but from the Church's sense of its own power.... People who think that the Scriptures should be the sole authority, should logically become 7th Day [Seventh-day] Adventists, and keep Saturday holy. ("Pastor's Page," *Sentinel*, Saint Catherine Catholic Church, Algonac, Michigan, May 21, 1995)

The Catholic Church is saying that if you want to belong to a church that stands solely on Scripture, you should become a Seventh-day Adventist. At the time I was studying I had never heard of the Seventh-day Adventist Church. It might seem strange, but I have to thank the Catholic Church for making it so clear to me that they follow man's traditions and man's laws.

Shortly thereafter I found out that my neighbor was a Seventh-day Adventist. I was so excited to meet someone from the church I felt followed the commandments of God. We started Bible studies, and everything I had studied on my own up until now was the same I was studying and learning about from my neighbor—Seventh-day Adventists keep the Sabbath, the seventh day of the week, and believe that through the power of Christ dwelling in you (the Holy Spirit) you can keep the commandments. This fit perfectly with what I had read in Revelation 12:17 and 14:12.

I was grateful for the friendship and guidance of my neighbor because I still had many questions. One was what will happen to those who worship on Sunday? I had met so many loving people in the Catholic Church and other churches. To find the answer, I turned to God's Word, and the Holy Spirit guided me to a parable in Luke.

> What man of you, having an hundred sheep, if he lose one of them, doth not leave the ninety and nine in the wilderness, and go after that which is lost, until he find it? And when he hath found it, he layeth it on his shoulders, rejoicing. And when he cometh home, he calleth together his friends and neighbours, saying unto them, Rejoice with me; for I have found my sheep which was lost. I say unto you, that likewise joy shall be in heaven over one sinner that repenteth, more than over ninety and nine just persons, which need no repentance. (Luke 15:4–7)

I had been a lost sheep, but God didn't give up on me. God didn't condemn me for what I did not know. Instead, He sought after me until I was ready to listen: "Awake to righteousness, and sin not; for some have not the knowledge of God: I speak this to your shame" (1 Cor. 15:34); "For God, who commanded the light to shine out of darkness, hath shined in our hearts, to give the light of the knowledge of the glory of God in the face of Jesus Christ" (2 Cor. 4:6). I took comfort in God's assurance that He has other sheep in other folds, people in other churches: "And other sheep I have, which are not of this fold: them also I must bring, and they shall hear my voice; and there shall be one fold, and one shepherd" (John 10:16).

> I had been a lost sheep, but God didn't give up on me. God didn't condemn me for what I did not know.

As long as we are growing in the knowledge of God's Word, we will be His people and will be partakers of His divine nature. We will be overcomers like Jesus: "To him that overcometh will I grant to sit with me in my throne, even as I also overcame, and am set down with my Father in his throne" (Rev. 3:21).

> Simon Peter, a servant and an apostle of Jesus Christ, to them that have obtained like precious faith with us through the righteousness of God and our Saviour Jesus Christ: Grace and peace be multiplied unto you through the knowledge of God, and of Jesus our Lord, according as his divine power hath given unto us all things that pertain unto life and godliness, through the knowledge of him that hath called us to glory and virtue: Whereby are given unto us exceeding great and precious promises: that by these ye might be partakers of the divine nature, having escaped the corruption that is in the world through lust. And beside this, giving

> all diligence, add to your faith virtue; and to virtue knowledge; and to knowledge temperance; and to temperance patience; and to patience godliness; and to godliness brotherly kindness; and to brotherly kindness charity. For if these things be in you, and abound, they make you that ye shall neither be barren nor unfruitful in the knowledge of our Lord Jesus Christ. (2 Peter 1:1–8)

In Revelation 14 I read about two groups of people. The one group is following the teachings of man and has rejected God's commandments. The other group has accepted Christ as their Savior and is preaching the everlasting gospel to those around them. They keep the commandments of God, including the Sabbath.

> And I saw another angel fly in the midst of heaven, having the everlasting gospel to preach unto them that dwell on the earth, and to every nation, and kindred, and tongue, and people, saying with a loud voice, Fear God, and give glory to him; for the hour of his judgment is come: and worship him that made heaven, and earth, and the sea, and the fountains of waters. And there followed another angel, saying, Babylon is fallen, is fallen, that great city, because she made all nations drink of the wine of the wrath of her fornication. And the third angel followed them, saying with a loud voice, If any man worship the beast and his image, and receive his mark in his forehead, or in his hand, the

> same shall drink of the wine of the wrath of God, which is poured out without mixture into the cup of his indignation; and he shall be tormented with fire and brimstone in the presence of the holy angels, and in the presence of the Lamb: And the smoke of their torment ascendeth up for ever and ever: and they have no rest day nor night, who worship the beast and his image, and whosoever receiveth the mark of his name. Here is the patience of the saints: here are they that keep the commandments of God, and the faith of Jesus. (Rev. 14:6–12)

As I studied, I longed to be found by God as a true Christian dedicated to His cause of reaching others and sharing with them God's call to His people in Revelation 18 to come out of the churches that teach false doctrines and to stand for the truth.

> And after these things I saw another angel come down from heaven, having great power; and the earth was lightened with his glory. And he cried mightily with a strong voice, saying, Babylon the great is fallen, is fallen, and is become the habitation of devils, and the hold of every foul spirit, and a cage of every unclean and hateful bird. For all nations have drunk of the wine of the wrath of her fornication, and the kings of the earth have committed fornication with her, and the merchants of the earth are waxed rich through the abundance of her delicacies.

> And I heard another voice from heaven, saying, Come out of her, my people, that ye be not partakers of her sins, and that ye receive not of her plagues. (Rev. 18:1–4)

The more I read the clearer it became that Christ is coming quickly and bringing His rewards with Him according to our works for those that keep the commandments of God and have the faith of Jesus. I look forward to that day!

> And I saw a new heaven and a new earth: for the first heaven and the first earth were passed away; and there was no more sea. And I John saw the holy city, new Jerusalem, coming down from God out of heaven, prepared as a bride adorned for her husband. And I heard a great voice out of heaven saying, Behold, the tabernacle of God is with men, and he will dwell with them, and they shall be his people, and God himself shall be with them, and be their God. And God shall wipe away all tears from their eyes; and there shall be no more death, neither sorrow, nor crying, neither shall there be any more pain: for the former things are passed away. And he that sat upon the throne said, Behold, I make all things new. And he said unto me, Write: for these words are true and faithful, and he said unto me, It is done. I am Alpha and Omega, the beginning and the end. I will give unto him that is athirst of the fountain of the water of life freely. He

that overcometh shall inherit all things; and I will be his God, and he shall be my son. (Rev. 21:1–7)

And he saith unto me, Seal not the sayings of the prophecy of this book: for the time is at hand. He that is unjust, let him be unjust still: and he which is filthy, let him be filthy still: and he that is righteous, let him be righteous still: and he that is holy, let him be holy still. And, behold, I come quickly; and my reward is with me, to give every man according as his work shall be. I am Alpha and Omega, the beginning and the end, the first and the last. Blessed are they that do his commandments, that they may have right to the tree of life, and may enter in through the gates into the city. (Rev. 22:10–14)

Chapter 7

Baptized and Sharing Jesus

My Christian life had begun. I was no longer living a nightmare; I was now walking with angels, still learning and always studying. I was thoroughly convinced and convicted of the truths of the Word of God, and I was ready to take my stand with the Sabbathkeeping people of God through baptism.

After joining the Seventh-day Adventist Church, I wanted to teach others about what I had learned as God called His disciples to do in Matthew 28:18–20: "And Jesus came and spake unto them, saying, All power is given unto me in heaven and in earth. Go ye therefore, and teach all nations, baptizing them in the name of the Father,

I was no longer living a nightmare; I was now walking with angels.

and of the Son, and of the Holy Ghost: Teaching them to observe all things whatsoever I have commanded you: and, lo, I am with you always, even unto the end of the world. Amen."

I committed myself to telling others about God's saving power. I went door to door; I gave Bible studies; I passed out religious pamphlets and books; and I shared my testimony with anyone who would listen. And God sent people to me who had problems or questions.

I could fill another book with the experiences I've had walking with God and His angels while sharing with others from God's Word, but I will only share a few stories in this last chapter. These experiences are not in order, and they feature good and bad encounters because that is life. As you share God's Word with others, you will find people who are happy to see you. Maybe they've prayed for someone to come and share God's Word with them. Many people are hurting for one reason or another. Maybe they've lost a loved one and need to be comforted through the promises of God's Word. God will open the doors for you to share, and you will be blessed as you share with others. Then there will be other times when you will be rejected, but God is still working on hearts.

I remember this one particular Bible study I had with a woman about the mark of the beast. I really did not want to do this study at this time, because we had only had three or four Bible studies previous to this. I prayed to God to guide me, and we set a time for the study. I didn't know that she had invited several members of her church, including her assistant pastor and an elder. The study went on for about four or five hours. No one said anything or questioned the Bible study at all. After I was done presenting the study, we all left for our homes. The next day I called her, and she said, "I never want to see you or study with you again." My heart broke, and I asked God to forgive me for saying so much. I didn't understand what had gone wrong since I had prayed for guidance.

One year later my brother-in-law and I were canvassing in the same area where I had had the Bible study. My brother-in-law knocked on her door, and somehow she thought to ask him if he was my brother-in-law. When he said yes, she told him she wanted to see me. I went to her house not knowing what she was going to do or say, but before I could say anything, she told me what had happened a year ago after the Bible study. "I just couldn't believe it. I had prayed to God to help me start studying again. I was not spending time in God's Word, and then He sent me you. I talked with my pastor, his assistant, and other church members in an effort to prove you wrong about the Sabbath being the seventh day of the week and not Sunday. I wanted them to show you that Sunday, the first day of the week, was blessed by God, but no one could. So, Bill, for this past year I have been studying to prove you wrong, but you were right. Saturday is the Sabbath."

I praised God that she had found the truth! It wasn't about me being right; it was about the truth of God's Word. God taught me a lesson that day. For a whole year I had blamed myself for not doing the Bible study the right way, but God had been working even though I couldn't see it. We may not always see how God is working on hearts, but we must trust Him. We are to do our part and let the Holy Spirit do His part.

Another time I shared my testimony with a friend at work, and then shortly after that I moved away from the area. I didn't see him for eight years. Then one day I was at Pacific Union College for a program, and I ran into my old friend and his wife. I asked them what they were doing there. He said, "Eight years ago when you shared your testimony with me it scared me so much that my wife and I began to study the Bible, and then we were baptized." Praise God! The last time I saw them they were getting ready to go overseas as missionaries.

When you share what God has done in your life, you can change lives. You may never know in this life how much your life has touched someone else, but some day in the kingdom you will.

Several years ago the Lord impressed me that I needed to see my little brother, so my wife and I made the three-hour drive to his home. We spent the whole day together and had a nice visit. Before we left we prayed together, and we left him a set of twenty-five videos from Amazing Facts. Two weeks later he died unexpectedly at the age of forty-eight. I asked his girlfriend if he had watched the videos, and she told me that he had watched them all within the first week after I had left them. That was at least two or more videos a day! Then she asked if she could have them to watch them also, so we gave her the set.

At my brother's funeral, God blessed me again and brought joy to my heart. There were a number of people saying he was in heaven, which is what most church's believe. Then I heard one woman telling some of the people there at the funeral that my brother was asleep in the ground, waiting for Jesus to come back at His second coming. After hearing this, I approached her and asked her what church she attended. "Bill, don't you remember me?" she asked. "Thirty years ago when I was seventeen years old you gave me a pamphlet, and it changed my life forever. I am a Seventh-day Adventist now."

Praise God! What a blessing to hear that giving a simple little pamphlet had made such a difference in her life. I didn't even remember giving her a pamphlet. I must have been in my twenties at the time I gave her the pamphlet. I was doing lots of door-to-door canvassing work and giving Bible studies to anyone who wanted to study.

There are so many things we can do for the Lord. God has blessed me with giving many Bible studies, some by mail and some in person.

Of course, when you go out door to door looking for people who want to have Bible studies, it's not always a good experience. There are times when people shout at you or slam the door in your face. I'd like to share a few of these bad experiences with you.

At this one house a man invited me to come in and show him the Bible books. He seemed really nice, so I went inside and sat on the couch as directed. However, as I started to show him the books, he told me to stop. Then another man came out of the back room, and they both stood in front of me. They started to threaten my life, telling me I wasn't going to leave there. I prayed to God for help and deliverance from this situation. I know God sent an angel, because after my prayer,

No one gets to my house past my dogs.

I got up and walked out the door while both men still stood in front of the couch.

Another time I had a bad experience was when I was working in a mountain community. I couldn't just go door to door on foot because the houses were sparsely scattered across the mountain, so I drove to each house. At one home after knocking on the door, a man ran out and flew past me. He looked around and then turned and questioned me as to how I had gotten in there. I really was not sure what he meant, but he kept saying, "How did you get here? No one gets to my house past my dogs." Then he called for his dogs, but they never came. I told him God had sent me to him, and that was how I had gotten there. He did not want anything to do with God. He said he would burn any lesson studies or any kind of Bible material I was thinking about leaving, so I left without leaving anything. I know God's angels watched over me that day.

Throughout my life God has always been there for me, watching over me. I know that many of us can say that we would not be alive today if it wasn't for God and His angels watching over us and saving our lives at times. This was the case in 1985 after I bought some land in the foothills of Oroville, California. The property was on a mountainside with a steep driveway. I needed a tractor to fix the road and do other work, so I bought a backhoe. It was really big with the bucket in front and the digger in the back. I unloaded it off the trailer that was parked across the driveway at the bottom of the hill. I drove it up the driveway and turned it around to go back down to park it in a clearing that was about halfway down the hill.

As I was going down the hill, the motor stopped, but the backhoe continued to roll down the driveway toward the trailer. I tried the brakes, but they wouldn't work. I thought if I could drop the bucket or the rear back digger it might slow me down, but nothing worked because the motor wasn't on. I was picking up speed and was almost to the bottom of the hill where the trailer was parked. There was nothing I could do but crash into the trailer. I thought that if I could hang on tight enough and not be thrown off I just might live. I braced myself, holding the steering wheel as tight as I could. Then I shut my eyes, called out to God for help, and waited for the impact. I kept waiting with my eyes shut, but I didn't hit anything. I opened my eyes and saw that the tractor had stopped about four inches from the trailer. There is no way the tractor could have stopped by itself unless God's angels stopped it. When we are walking with God and doing His will, we are walking with angels.

Some of the stories bring tears to my eyes as I am writing about them. One involved an uncle of mine who was very sick. He was dying from cancer and was in a lot of pain. About two weeks before he died, we prayed that he would have no pain. He wasn't worried about dying; he just didn't want the pain. Just before he died, we were sitting on some steps. I was holding him up waiting for the ambulance to come. I prayed for him, and he looked up at me and smiled and said, "There's no pain." Praise God!

I was giving a woman Bible studies, and she wanted to be baptized, but every Friday night to Saturday night she got so sick she could not get out of bed. I and the pastor and elder went to her home one Friday evening and anointed her and prayed for her to be healed. The next morning she was at church and was baptized. She never got sick again on Sabbath. Praise God!

One day I received a letter from a young woman saying she wanted someone to visit her. I could hardly read her writing. She said she was dying and was afraid to die. I was so busy with Bible studies, visitations, and other church related work that it was a month and a half or more before I got to her house. It was too late. She had passed away. My heart was broken. I prayed and asked God to forgive me, and I promised Him that day that if I ever got another letter like that again I would go right away to visit that person. I've kept my promise.

There was another man I came in contact with who was dying of cancer, but let me start from the beginning of the story. I was giving Bible studies to a woman, and after the second Bible study she asked me if she could have an extra copy of the study. I was happy to give her the extra copy. This continued, her asking me for extra copies of the studies until we got about halfway through the series of studies. One day I finally asked her what she was doing with the other studies. She said she had a neighbor, a young girl in her twenties who she was giving them to. God impressed me that I needed to meet her, so the woman I was studying with introduced us.

The young woman started telling me about her dad who was dying from cancer. She told me she wanted to let her dad know how much she loved him, but he didn't want to see anyone. For several years she and her dad had not been speaking to each other. She had been praying that God would send someone to her. She said I was an answer to her prayers. She gave me the address where her dad lived and asked me to let him know that she loved and forgave him. She wanted to be there for him to the end. I told her I would deliver the message for her.

The next day I went to her dad's house. He should have been home, but he wasn't. I knew he could not drive or get around very well. Then a thought came to my mind that I should go to the hospital. As I walked through the doors of the hospital, I passed a man walking out. We both stopped, turned around, and looked at each other. We had never met before, so we didn't know each other. This man could not talk, or eat, because his throat had been burned from radiation treatments. As we walked up to each other, he gave me a big hug. He then took out a notebook and wrote, "God sent you to me." Then he wrote again, "For the last hour I've been trying to get a ride home, but couldn't."

Then he realized that God really had sent me to him. I took him home and told him how much his daughter loved him. He was very thankful and wanted to see her to let her know that he had never stopped loving her. When I told her about her father's response, she broke down in tears. Every week for the next four months, I met with her dad to pray with him and have Bible studies. He had never prayed before and didn't know how. I told him to just talk to God as to a father and end the prayer by saying, "In the name of Jesus Christ, Amen." Before this man died, he gave his heart to Jesus, and he wrote that he was at peace.

One day while I was at work, a woman came up to me and asked if I remembered the young girl who used to work at the check-in gate? That had been more than ten years ago that this young girl had worked there. Then the woman told me that this young girl was dying of cancer at the Center for Cancer in San Francisco. She asked me if I could go and see her. I didn't need to go looking for people to share the love of God with, God sent them to me! I went to see her, and we prayed together. She was happy I came. I asked her to tell me about her cancer. She said, "About a year and four months ago I got cancer. I went through all the treatments, and it went into remission for a year. Then it came back, so I did another round of treatments, but this time it went into remission for only two months. Then it came back the third time. I took more treatments, but again after being in remission for only two months it came back. Now, it's back for the fourth time, and I'm in the hospital undergoing treatments, and this time the cancer is not going away." Then she said, "Bill, we just bought a house, we have two young daughters, and I don't want to die!"

I asked her what she ate and drank. She said she drank a lot of sodas and ate a lot of meat and fast food. I told her to continue going through her cancer treatment but that she had to change her diet too. She had to stop drinking sodas and eating meat and fast food. I told her she needed to eat a plant-based diet consisting of fresh fruits and vegetables along with drinking lots of water and certain teas. I also told her to pray and give her life to God. She followed the plan I gave her. It's been more than ten years now and the cancer has never come back. Praise God!

I have many more stories like these, which I call my treasures in heaven. I'm just an average person like everyone else. I'm nobody special, except maybe to God and my loved ones. I have experienced my share of heartache and pain of a broken home and lost loved ones. There are times I feel like I can't go on, or I feel like I just don't want to go on, but God pulls me through.

This reminds me of a family I know and a good friend whom I miss very much. He was a lay evangelist working on a Bible project that took him all over the world. His two oldest boys always wanted to go with him, but he always said it was too dangerous for them to come. Then on his last mission journey he gave in to their pleadings. After flying into the main airport, they had to take a small private airplane to their final destination. The meetings went very well. People's hearts were turned to God. Unfortunately, on the return trip the private airplane crashed. He and his two sons along with the pilot and another passenger were all killed. I thought of his wife and his little girl and youngest son. I prayed for God to comfort them and give them strength, and also to be with the other family members.

> It's been more than ten years now and the cancer has never come back.

At the funeral I tried to think of what I could say to his wife to comfort her and the rest of the family, but there were no words that I could think of. I'll never forget what his wife said to me when I gave her a hug. She said, "Bill, I don't understand why, but the real question is, do I trust Him?"

I have had to ask myself that question many times. Do you trust God? When you are sick. When a loved one is dying. When you lose a child in an accident. Do you trust Him? When you lose your job, and you can't pay the bills. Do you trust Him? When you lose your family in a divorce, your home, and everything you have worked for. Do you trust Him? The answer is YES! We may not always understand, but we have a God who loves us more than anything. He gave us His own Son, Jesus Christ, to give us a way back to Him. Christ allows tests and trials to strengthen our faith in Him. He never leaves us during these times; instead, He goes through the tests and trials with us.

In the following verses Christ tells us that He is preparing a place for us and will soon come back to take us home. "Let not your heart be troubled: ye believe in God, believe also in me. In my Father's house are many mansions: if it were not so, I would have told you. I go to prepare a place for you. And if I go and prepare a place for you, I will come again, and receive you unto myself; that where I am, there ye may be also. And whither I go ye know, and the way ye know. Thomas saith unto him, Lord, we know not whither thou goest; and how can we know the way? Jesus saith unto him, I am the way, the truth, and the life: no man cometh unto the Father, but by me" (John 14:1–6).

> I don't understand why, but the real question is, do I trust Him?

Christ is the only way. I am forever grateful to my Savior for rescuing me from the grip of Satan and pointing me toward the cross. It is my prayer that my struggle and surrender to God will inspire you to give your life to Him today.

www.ingramcontent.com/pod-product-compliance
Lightning Source LLC
Chambersburg PA
CBHW060442090426
42733CB00011B/2361
* 9 7 8 1 4 7 9 6 0 3 5 5 8 *